79p

How to Play Chess

Emanuel Lasker

with an introduction by W. H. Watts

Cadogan Books

London

This edition published 1995 by Cadogan Books plc, London House, Parkgate Road, London, SW11 4NQ

ISBN 1 85744 177 X

Printed and bound in Finland by Werner Söderström Oy

CONTENTS

Introduction   *1*
  I   The Rules of Chess   5
  II The Initial Position   8
  III The Pieces   10
  IV Notation Systems   11
  V   The Moves of the Pieces   15
  VI Exercises   18
  VII The Object of the Game   20
  VIII Exercises   22
  IX The End Game   30
  X   The Start of the Game   50
  XI Principles of Chess Strategy   57
  XII Examples of the Play of Masters,
      with Explanatory Notes   76
  The Chess World   105

INTRODUCTION

EVERYONE will admit Dr. Emanuel Lasker's pre-eminent skill as an exponent of Chess play. Many writers have endeavoured to discover from his games the secret of his success, and the conclusions at which they arrive are by no means alike. He does not appear to see more deeply into any given position than other masters, his combinations are not more subtle nor are they more subtly timed than those of his opponents. His play is not more sound, in fact the late Richard Réti goes so far as to say that Lasker deliberately made moves that were unsound and which he knew were not the best moves in order that his opponent might be tempted into a faulty plan or a losing variation. On this question Dr. Lasker maintains a discreet silence and for those players who desire only an average skill such academic discussion is far too abstruse. Whatever his method in the course of his professional career as a player the result has abundantly justified it. His measure of success will long remain without equal and it seems almost certain that it will not be possible for any player of the future to retain the world's championship title for twenty-six years, as Lasker did.

1

Unlike many other famous players his tournament record and his results in individual matches are equally brilliant. In a long list of International Tournaments from 1888 to 1924 he was never placed lower than 3rd and in a large majority of cases was a clear first. In individual matches over the same period he won all but three—two of these were short matches and were both drawn, and the third was his match with Capablanca which he lost.

Dr. Lasker's record of accomplishment for Chess, his writings and his research, and many of his games which will last for all time, make him, like Chess itself, an international possession. He is removed from the prejudices of mere Nationalism because the Chess players of Great Britain, America, France, Russia, and every other country, benefit without distinction from his life's work.

It does not follow that pre-eminence as a player carries with it exceptional abilities as a teacher, and to re-assure ourselves on this point we must turn to Dr. Lasker's writings on the game. His earliest and perhaps best known book is "Common Sense in Chess" and this book alone provides sufficient answer to our enquiry. It is a reprint of a series of lectures (lessons) given to a group of London players many years ago. It has gone through several editions both in this country and abroad and has been translated into many languages.

The book by which he is best known, however, is his "Manual of Chess," and in this he has endeavoured to supply the modern Chess world with an adequate and fitting substitute for Staunton's Handbook which had held undisputed sway for over fifty years. Whether he has succeeded or not it will be for posterity to say. He certainly has proved that Chess is more than a mere game or pastime, which was all that Staunton thought it was and without exception contemporary authorities have acclaimed Lasker's Manual as a masterpiece.

With the present work the great player has successfully assumed the rôle of a great teacher and in so doing he has adopted and improved a method of instruction which although common in many other subjects has not previously been used by teachers of Chess. The method appealed to me instantly because in some small measure it was the method I had used when teaching beginners. In fact I remember one pupil of mine who could checkmate me with unerring precision with King, Knight and Bishop against my lone King long before he knew how the other pieces moved.

My principle was to teach the movements of one piece and then a second piece. Then learn to combine the two and when this was grasped add a third and so on until the pupil was ready to start playing his first game. In fact it likens the teaching of Chess to teaching to play the piano.

A position, invented by Sam Loyd, is so very useful and instructive that it might be well to include it here.

1.—Place the Black King so that White, playing, may Mate on the move.

2.—Place the Black King where, having the move, he is Stalemated.

By S. Loyd

3.—Place the Black King where, having the move, he stands Checkmated.

There is no limit to positions of the kind used by Dr. Lasker and the ingenious teacher can invent new ones at will which serve to impress the points at issue still more conclusively upon the mind of the pupil. Thus the teaching method is a progressive one and leads the pupil from complete ignorance of the game, with increasing interest by a logical course to a comprehensive grasp of the powers of all the pieces both individually and in combination with each other. He is then in a position to learn the Principles and to start playing, and when he arrives at this stage he is ready, in fact anxious, to continue his studies, which he can best do with the aid of "Lasker's Manual of Chess."

W. H. WATTS

THE RULES OF CHESS

EVERYONE should know chess, because the mentality and individuality of the human race has found expression in this game in its modern development. To try to understand its aspirations and to comprehend what masters and thinkers have given to mankind is a tribute to the genius of the human race.

This end can be attained easily, provided the right method of learning is followed.

Chess originated from warfare. In olden times two armies opposed to each other took up their positions in nearly straight lines, separated by a nearly level plane. A general, to make his plans clear to his officers, sketched the position and indicated movements of bodies of men. In this way military games such as chess, were generated. Possibly Hannibal before the battle of Cannæ drew lines and placed stones on a board to explain his intended strategy for that battle. In this instance it is easily comprehended, as shown by the two drawings on *p.* 6:

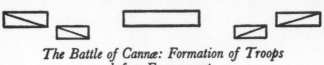

*The Battle of Cannæ: Formation of Troops
before Engagement.*

*The Battle of Cannæ, showing the strategy employed
by the Carthaginians.*

Battle of Cannæ

216 B.C.

ROMANS;	Infantry	▬	*80,000*
	Cavalry	◪	*6,000*
CARTHAGINIANS;	Infantry	▭	*40,000*
	Cavalry	◪	*10,000*

These lines describe a plan which made history

For the purpose of teaching strategy, the battlefield was represented by the chessboard. It was given the shape of a square, divided into 64 squares, usually coloured White and Black alternately.

The Chessboard

THE INITIAL POSITION

CHESS is a game played between two opponents, distinguished as White and Black. Each player is provided with sixteen men, all of the same colour, White or Black. Eight of each group are called pawns, the other eight are called pieces. At the commencement of a game each player places his sixteen men on the board in a definite order. The eight pieces are the King, here indicated by a King's crown; the Queen, here shown by a Queen's crown; two Castles or Rooks, which appear in the diagram as Castles; two Bishops, each depicted by a Bishop's mitre, and two Knights, indicated by the heads of horses. The eight Pawns are printed as so many small men.

In the initial position the Rook in White's left hand corner is called Queen's Rook, abbreviated QR. The one in White's right-hand corner, King's Rook, KR. Similarly, Queen's Knight is written QKt, King,s Knight KKt, Queen's Bishop QB, King's Bishop KB' Queen Q, and King K. The pawns are named after the pieces in front of which they are placed. The King's Pawn, KP, is the one in front of the K, etc. The White

The Initial Position of the 32 Men on the Board

Army is classified into the Queen's side or the left wing, and the King's side or the right wing. The Black Army is classified in the same way, the Black Q is placed opposite the White Q, the Black K opposite the White K. The Black QR opposite the White QR, etc., but Black's left wing is opposite White's right wing. Therefore Black's left wing is his King's side. The square in the bottom right-hand corner is always a white one. The Q stands on a square of her own colour the White Q on a white square, the Black Q on a black one, when the pieces are placed on the board for the commencement of play.

THE PIECES

IN THE course of the game the players change the position of their pieces according to certain rules. They "move" a man from its square to another square. No two men are ever allowed to stand on the same square. Whenever a man is moved to a square occupied by a hostile man the hostile piece is "captured" and removed from the board. The players "move" alternately and White makes the first "move."

As has already been explained, each army consists of sixteen different men: King, Queen, Castle or Rook (2), Bishop (2), Knight (2), Pawn (8). They move differently, as will presently be explained.

♜♞♝♛ IV ♚♝♞♜

NOTATION SYSTEMS

SINCE we shall have to speak of the 64 squares of the board, we shall have to use some form of notation which will briefly but clearly indicate what we mean, and the individual square under discussion. The need for such a notation has been felt ever since the first book was written on chess, but as yet authorities are not agreed as to the best system. There are two systems in vogue, the one is scientific and abstract, the other descriptive and concrete, probably the former will win in the end. The scientific notation is based on "co-ordinates."

Looking at the board from White's side, the eight files of the board from left to right are designated by the eight letters **a, b, c, d, e, f, g, h,** and the eight ranks on the board from the lower to the upper side are denoted by the eight numbers **1, 2, 3, 4, 5, 6, 7, 8.** A square is named by the use of both its file letter and rank number, for instance, e1 is the square where the White King stands in the initial position, d8 the one where the Black Queen stands in the initial position. This notation is in use in many countries, but is of rather recent origin. Earlier in the history of the game another notation was generally in use, and some countries have stuck to it, mainly the English-speaking countries and the Latin countries. In this form the eight files from left to right are called the Queen's Rook's file, or QR file; the Queen's Knight's file, or QKt file; the Queen's Bishop's file, or QB file; the Queen's or Q file; the King's or K file; the King's Bishop's or KB file; the King's Knight's or KKt file; the King's Rook's or KR file. The square on which a piece in the initial position stands is called

BLACK

8	a8	b8	c8	d8	e8	f8	g8	h8
7	a7	b7	c7	d7	e7	f7	g7	h7
6	a6	b6	c6	d6	e6	f6	g6	h6
5	a5	b5	c5	d5	e5	f5	g5	h5
4	a4	b4	c4	d4	e4	f4	g4	h4
3	a3	b3	c3	d3	e3	f3	g3	h3
2	a2	b2	c2	d2	e2	f2	g2	h2
1	a1	b1	c1	d1	e1	f1	g1	h1
	a	b	c	d	e	f	g	h

WHITE

The Chessboard in algebraic or scientific notation

by the name of the piece, for instance, King's square, abbreviated K or K1, etc., and the squares in front of each piece are indicated by their file and their distance from the base. Thus K4 is the square on the King's file fourth from the base or K sq., which must be included in the counting. Moreover, in this form

BLACK

	KR	KKt	KB	Q	K	QB	QKt	QR	
8	QR8	QKt8	QB8	Q8	K8	KB8	KKt8	KR8	1
7	QR7	QKt7	QB7	Q7	K7	KB7	KKt7	KR7	2
6	QR6	QKt6	QB6	Q6	K6	KB6	KKt6	KR6	3
5	QR5	QKt5	QB5	Q5	K5	KB5	KKt5	KR5	4
4	QR4	QKt4	QB4	Q4	K4	KB4	KKt4	KR4	5
3	QR3	QKt3	QB3	Q3	K3	KB3	KKt3	KR3	6
2	QR2	QKt2	QB2	Q2	K2	KB2	KKt2	KR2	7
1	QR1	QKt1	QB1	Q1	K1	KB1	KKt1	KR1	8

QR	QKt	QB	Q	K	KB	KKt	KR

WHITE

The Chessboard in the descriptive notation from White's point of view

If you turn the book upside down you will see the board from Black's point of view as numbered by him in the descriptive notation.

of notation, the squares have a double designation according to the point of view of the player. Black, in recording his move, calculates from his own point of view, denotes the files in the same way as White, but the squares by their distance from his own base line.

The chessboard in the descriptive notation from Black's point of view is the same as this one except that Black takes the place of White, and conversely. The square **K1** from White's point of view is **K8** from Black's point of view, and conversely.

If White begins the game by moving the pawn from **e2** to **e4** and Black replies **e7** to **e5**, the moves are written algebraically:

1 e2–e4   e7–e5

and in the descriptive notation:

1 **P–K4**   **P–K4**

All signs, hereafter to be explained, of which the chess language makes use, belong to the two systems of notation equally. A sign of multiplication means a capture, **O–O** means Castling with the King's Rook, **O–O–O** Castling with the Queen's Rook. A cross † means a threat to capture the King, also called Check, abbreviated ch. A double threat to capture the King is called "Double Check." Checkmate is written ‡. A mark of exclamation "!" set after a move denotes an excellent move, or the best move. A question mark "?" set after a move means that the move is at least questionable or downright bad, a mistake or blunder. Two question marks "??" set after a move accentuate that criticism.

♖♘♗♕ V ♚♝♞♜

THE MOVES OF THE PIECES

THE King moves to any square adjoining his own, unoccupied by a man of his side. He is, however, debarred from moving to a square where he is exposed to capture and cannot occupy any square next to the other King. In moving the King to a square occupied by a hostile man the player captures that piece. In certain cases the King and the Castle move at the same time. That move is called "Castling," and will be fully described later on. Place the White King on d4, the Black King on d6. White then has the choice of five legal moves.

The Rook moves from its square on to any square in the same rank or file, provided it encounters no obstruction. Place a White Castle on c2, the White King on f2, the Black King on g7. If it is White's turn to play he has the choice between 19 legal moves (the Castle cannot go to f2, or g2, or h2). The King can execute eight legal moves, the Castle eleven. With the move of the Castle from c2 to c7, White "checks," i.e., threatens to capture the Black King next move.

The Bishop moves from his square to any square in his diagonal provided he encounters no obstruction.

Place the Bishop on c4, he can execute eleven legal moves. He may, for instance, move to f7, or f1. A White Pawn on b3 would obstruct the squares a2 and b3. A Black Pawn on e6 could be captured by the B but would obstruct f7 and g8.

The Queen may make any move that a Rook or a Bishop are able to make—Place a White Queen on d4. If White resolves to move the Q he has the choice between twenty-seven legal moves.

The Pawn moves one step forward, except in its initial position, when it may move one or two steps at will. If the square in front of the Pawn is occupied the Pawn is "blocked," and cannot move forward at all until the obstruction has been removed. The Pawn captures a hostile man placed one step diagonally forward. This rule is modified by the capture "*en passant*" or in passing. If a Pawn by moving two steps from its initial position passes an enemy Pawn standing on its own fifth rank, on either of the next adjoining files, the latter Pawn, provided it wants to avail itself of the privilege on the next move, has the right to capture the hostile Pawn *en passant*, which capture is effected in just the same way as if the hostile Pawn had moved only one step. A Pawn that by any route has reached the eighth rank of the board ceases to be a Pawn. In that moment it has to be changed into a piece of its own colour, barring solely the King, and this rule holds good even though a piece should have to be supplied from another box. Examples will be given later on.

The Knight moves on to any square not occupied

by a man on each side that it can reach by proceeding in any direction two squares on its rank or file and one square at right angles thereto. If a square that it can thus reach is occupied by a hostile man the Knight may capture that man by placing itself on that square —from d4 the Kt can make eight moves, from c2 six moves. Thus it will be seen that the Kt always moves to a square of the other colour to that on which it stands.

Castling is a move executed by King and Rook simultaneously. The conditions under which the move is allowed are as follows:

1. Neither King nor Rook shall have moved before in that game.

2. The squares on the rank between King and Rook must be unoccupied.

3. In Castling, neither the K nor the R are permitted to expose themselves to capture, nor may the K Castle to get out of check. In other words, neither the square which the K leaves, nor the one over which he passes, nor the one to which he goes may be under attack from a hostile piece.

4. The King must move along the rank two squares, either to right or left as the case may be, and the R which is approached, jumps over the K to the square contiguous thereto.*

* *So as to avoid ambiguity the K should be moved first or the two pieces simultaneously.*

EXERCISES

1. It is advisable to practise with a friend and to invent exercises, for instance: How many different moves can the White pawn on **c2** make in the position—WHITE: **K** on **c3**, **P** on **c2**; BLACK: **K** on **c5**, **B** on **d3**?

One move. It can capture the Bishop. It cannot advance straight forward because it is blocked.

2. What points are accessible in one move to a White **Kt** on **QKt3**, the White **K** being placed on **QB5** with no other White man on the board?

The five points: **QR1, QB1, Q2, Q4, QR5.**

3. The position is WHITE: **K** on **QB1**, **P** on **Q2**; BLACK: **K** on his **K4**, **P** on his **K5** and his **K7**. White to play moves *1* P—Q4 check.

Black can capture the pawn in two ways, by the K or by taking it *en passant.*

4. WHITE: **K** on **QR1**, **R** on **QKt2**, **B** on **QKt1**, **Ps** on **QR2, QR3**; BLACK: **K** on **QR5** (White's **QR4**),

Q on **QB6**, **R** on **QB8**. White to play. How many legal moves can White make?

None, he is not permitted to expose his K. His Ps are blocked.

5. What is the shortest number of moves in which a **Kt** on **b2** can occupy **f8**?

Four moves. It can accomplish that journey within that time in various ways. Find them out.

....

THE OBJECT OF THE GAME

THE object of the player is to capture the hostile King by force or, if that cannot be accomplished, at least to defeat the attempt of the opponent to effect the capture of his own King. A move which menaces capture of the King is called "check." If the opponent cannot defend the King against the check it is termed "check and mate," or "Checkmate," or, still more briefly, "mate." These words originate from Persia. Check means Shah, monarch, and mate signifies death.

Put the following positions up on the board and make sure that you understand both the positions and the explanations appended to each:

WHITE: **K** on **g1, R** on **e8**; BLACK: **K** on **g8**, pawns on **f7, g7, h7**. Black is check and mate, or mated.

WHITE: **K b1, Q f6**; BLACK: **K g8, Q b2**, pawn **c3**. White is mated.

WHITE: **K e1, Rs** on **a7** and **b7**; BLACK: **Kg8, Rs g2**, and **c1**. White is mated.

WHITE: **K a1**; BLACK: **K g8, Q c2.** White to play has no legal move, but he is not in check, he therefore does not lose the game. It ends then and there as a drawn battle. The mate is "stale"—a "stalemate."

Games often end by agreement. A player "resigns" because he considers his position is indefensible. Two players agree to draw because neither entertains a hope of being able to force a win. When players do not terminate the contest by agreement they have to continue playing until one of the following situations arises:

Checkmate: The party whose King has been check-mated loses the game.

Stalemate: The party whose turn it is to move has no legal move left, but whose King is not in check, is no worse off than the opposing party. Such game is drawn.

Repetition of moves: After the same position has thrice arisen, the same party to play each time, the game is drawn.

Fifty Moves rule: After any successive fifty moves which have produced no marked change in the position the game is drawn. A marked change is brought about only by checkmate, stalemate, a capture or a pawn's move.

EXERCISES

1. Black is in check. He cannot capture the checking piece nor can he interpose but must move his K. Then White captures the Rook on f4.

2. White is in Check and as he cannot capture the checking piece, move his King out of the line of the attacking piece, nor legally interpose one of his own pieces, he is checkmated. In other words the game is over and White has lost.

3. Show how it is that Black has lost.

4. Say whose turn it is to move and if the game is finished state the result.

5. Neither the White K or either of his Rs has been moved in this game.

White to play can Castle Q side, but may not Castle K side. Why?

6. WHITE: **K c1, R g6, P f7;** BLACK: **K h7, Q h8, Kt g8.** White to play, wins. How?

By f7–f8, promotes the P to a Kt and mates.

7. WHITE: **K on KKt1, Q on K6, Kt on KB7;** BLACK: **K on KKt1, Rs on QR1 and K1, Ps on KKt2, KR2.** White to play. He moves *1* Kt–KR6, that is check by the Kt as well as "discovered" check by the Q, a "double check," in reply to which Black must move his K. Why? Show also how White wins.

8. WHITE: **K on KKt6, Q on QR2, R on QKt1;** BLACK: **K on KR1, R on QR1, B on KKt7, P on KKt2.** What would Black do if White played Q x R *ch?* What advantage does White gain by that sacrifice?

9. WHITE: **Kt on K4;** BLACK: **K on K1.** Can the White Kt by making an appropriate move say check? It can.

In how many different ways? In two ways.

Point out the two moves that give check.

10. WHITE: **R on K1, Kt on K4;** BLACK: **K on K1, Q on Q1, B on KB1, P on KB2.** White to move his Kt and checkmate the Black King by means of a double check.

11. WHITE: **K on KR1, P on KB7;** BLACK: **K on KR2, Q on KKt3, Ps on KKt2 and KR3.** White to play and say check and win the Black Queen.

12. WHITE: **Q on QKt3, Kt on KKt5;** BLACK: **K on K1, Q on Q1.** White to play and mate.

The student should invent similar exercises for himself until he becomes completely familiar with all the movements of all the pieces.

THE TWOFOLD METHOD

1. The reflection which follows is no digression from the pursuit of our main subject. It belongs to the idea, the plan, the mission of chess, although it refers to no move, nor to any particular position. If chess was not invented to elucidate the twofold method with which we shall deal presently, it certainly does elucidate it in a multitude of instances, and exceedingly well.

This method can be applied wherever man attempts to achieve a set purpose. It teaches him to approach his object in two different ways: Firstly, by concentrating his attention on the end, secondly by paying heed solely to the needs of the present.

These two procedures are opposed to each other. He who successfully reasons out the move necessary to achieve the end in view has solved the task set him. The man who successfully meets the needs of the present is not certain of the future and may be disappointed by the final results. On the other hand, he who goes the sure way has an immense labour to perform, whereas he who is satisfied with discovering only the next step to take has an easy task.

2. To apply the first procedure by itself we have to visualise the end and to deduce the means of attaining it. In the process of deduction we have to consider every possibility. The number of possibilities in chess sometimes runs into millions of millions of millions. Naturally we cannot follow this procedure except in positions presenting a small number of possibilities, but if we apply the second procedure by itself we may miss a shortcut to victory, and, though improving our chances all the time, ultimately attain no more than a draw. Consequently we must make a synthesis of the two procedures.

The question is perhaps illuminated by the following imaginary example: A treasure seeker knows that in a certain locality there exists a treasure, access to which is defended by many guards. To obtain the treasure he has to approach it and to overcome or to evade the guards which he meets on the way. He will be well advised to improve his chances step by step. After having approached his object sufficiently, the tactics of proceeding step by step would lead him no further. He must now ascertain the exact place which holds the treasure and consider whether he should attack the few guards which still separate him from it. If his force is equal to this task, provided he chooses the line of least resistance, he must attack unhesitatingly. If his force is not equal to this task he must first gather more strength. To arrive at a decision he has to apply deduction intelligently. He can do so because after he has approached his object, the number of possibilities to be investigated, which at the start of his adventure was enormous, is reduced now to only a few.

3. The outcome of a move is often uncertain because we cannot take all possibilities into consideration. Man is too frail. Life is too short for such a task. Therefore we have often to be content with the commonsense procedure of strengthening our force so as to be ready to meet unforeseen emergencies, but in positions which we can completely analyse we should attempt to arrive at deductions because analysis is definite and convincing, and in that respect superior to commonsense.

4. Every chess player has his own individual way of applying analysis and commonsense. There are two extreme types, the one aiming at security and knowledge, the other at novelty and adventure. The one type relies on memory and logic, the other on his judgment. The former is called a book player, the second a natural player.

I want to teach my pupil how to become primarily a natural player who burdens his memory very little, who applies logic only when deduction is called for, and who has a ready judgment to back him up in novel situations, for the natural player is a better type of man than the book player. The book player follows the standard of games played by masters, and, to do so, must commit to memory a large number of isolated facts. The natural player relies on his judgment and he must cultivate a sure and capable judgment or else he will fail. In life isolated facts are of small account, whereas a sure and capable judgment is needed

on all sides. Very great masters are always natural
players, and all those who desire to make themselves
strong in life, which implies that they use their memory
with economy, should train their judgment.

5. The pursuit of an objective has to be conducted
from two points, the beginning and the finish. A clear
conception of the final operations is essential to him
who wants to foresee, whereas he who is adventurous,
who desires to plunge into a sea of possibilities because he is self-reliant and circumspect, is quick to
detect the next step to be followed though he be ig-
norant as to where it may lead him. The two ways are
equally meritorious, they have to be judiciously combined, and we shall here follow both of them in turn
and explain as far as we can their peculiar condition
and adaption.

The compass of him who reflects on the end in view
is logical reasoning, he has to visualise the various
checkmates, and the processes to produce them or to
prevent them. His reasoning has to proceed step by
step, like a demonstration of one of Euclid's propositions. The compass of the adventurous mind which
starts on a voyage into unknown regions is the judgment of values. The effect of the pieces, the work which
they actually do, as well as that which they are expected
to do later on, guides his enterprise. He has to estimate
that effect and to abide by his estimates; if they are
wrong he is beaten, but he will not abandon his method
on that account. To err is his hazard, and to learn from
error is part of his method. He will continue to try,

and, while his success grows he will continue occasionally to fail and to learn. With relatively little trouble he approximates to truth, content not to obtain its full measure, whereas his antagonist, who desires to attain certainty by deduction and disdains anything but perfection, is liable to lose himself among the numerous possibilities and to jump too readily at conclusions which do not stand the test.

THE END GAME

WE BEGIN by asking and considering the question how a game of chess is to be won. The King may be mated though supported by many of his men; the pawns may march onward, and, by becoming pieces, overwhelm the opponent; a slight advantage may be gained, the forces of the opponent may be systematically worn down and in the end the advantage made to tell. The latter process, often combined with the second one, constitutes what chess players are wont to call the "End Game." The smallest advantage sufficient to win a game is that of a Rook. King and Rook opposed by a lone King, provided it is their move, can always force a checkmate. This is the most fundamental fact of the End Game. The procedure is as follows:

To begin with the Rook if attacked by the hostile King is brought into safety, secondly the adverse K is limited in its range of action and that range narrowed down until it is reduced to the edge of the board, finally the K is there driven into a mating position.

We begin to demonstrate these three processes by

starting with the last one. The checkmate by King
and Rook on the edge of the board is possible. Put a
Black King anywhere and a White King as near to it
as legally possible; you will then have the two Kings
in a position where they exert the strongest effect upon
each other. That figure is called "Opposition." The

effect upon each other consists in the restriction of
their possible movements since they are not allowed
to be on contiguous squares, to go there would be
suicide of the offender, and a K is not permitted to
sacrifice himself. They obstruct each other when in
opposition to the extent of each losing three squares
(in exceptional cases one or two only) of the K's region
of mobility. This conceded we see the maximum
effect of K and R against the adverse K does not
suffice to achieve the mate as long as that K is in the
centre, but if that K is on the edge of the board the
maximum effect of K and R against it just suffices for
the mate.

To force the Black K into one of these positions K
and R of the aggressor have to co-operate, they have

to drive the adverse K to the edge of the board. To do so methodically they have to restrict the adverse King's mobility so as to force him towards the edge. The opponent's right to move is also an obligation, and for this obligation the German term "*Zugzwang*" has been internationally adopted. The K can be forced into a position in which he must abandon his present position for a less favourable one. Take as an instance the following diagram which shows only the squares that matter.

Black here restricts White as much as he can. Obliged to move he is under the necessity of taking up a position of less effect. The game might thus proceed 1 . . . , K–Kt1; 2 K–Kt6, K–R1; 3 R–B8, or else *1* . . . , **K–R2**; *2* **R–Kt6**, **K–R1**; *3* **K–B6**,

K–R2; *4* **K–B7, K–R1;** *5* **R–R6.** A similar play en-
sues after 1 . . . , **K–R1;** *2* **K–Kt6.**

At the start of the drive the K and his R are not
likely to be in co-operation, they may be distant from
each other and from the adverse K. In that case they
have to advance methodically so as to restrict the
adverse K in his mobility and to get into touch with
each other, that done the drive may begin in earnest.
If for instance the initial position is as follows:

White commences with R–R4, so that the R re‧
stricts the Black K, who will henceforth have no
opportunity of passing over White's fourth line, provided the R maintains its guard and is protected
against capture. After this the White K will hurry to
the scene of action: *1* **R–R4, K–K4;** *2* **K–K2, K–Q4;**
3 **K–K3, K–B4;** *4* **R–Q4, K–B3;** *5* **K–Q3, K–B4;**
6 **K–B3, K–B3;** *7* **K–B4, K–Kt3;** *8* **R–Q6** *ch.* Here
a check is useful but it is an exceptional case. *8* . . . ,
K–B2; *9* **K–B5.** The end is now in sight.

The logic of the End Game K and R versus K applies also in the cases K and two B's versus K; and K, B and Kt versus K. The reader may use the very same course of reasoning to demonstrate the following propositions:

For K and Kt against K no mating position exists, nor for K and B versus K. With K and two B's the adverse K is easily forced into a mate on the edge of the board or preferably in a corner. With K and B and Kt against K, mating positions exist on the edge but the adverse K can successfully resist the attempt of being driven into such mate, with the sole exception of the corner of the same colour as the B. With K and two Kts against K mating positions exist on the edge of the board, but the attempt to drive the K into such a position, if intelligently disputed, always fails.

To illuminate and exemplify these statements a

Black to play and draw   *Which is the right move for Black?*

If White plays Kt–Kt5, Black is Stalemate. What other moves have the same effect?

White to play and mate

few positions are here indicated, the message of which may be easily understood.

White being set the task with K, B and Kt to drive the adverse K into a corner must make use of the maximum co-operation of his three pieces. The B takes effect on squares of one colour only, because in moving diagonally he always dominates squares of the same colour. Therefore in order not to duplicate the effect of the B, the K and Kt must work on those flight squares of the adverse K that are not of the colour dominated by the B. In this manner the flight of the adverse K is restricted so that he can be driven towards the edge of the board. For instance:

1 **Kt–K7, K–B3;** *2* **B–K3.** The B cuts off the flight square KKt4, the Kt the squares KB4 and KKt3. The White K exerts the strongest effect due to his being in "opposition." *2* . . . , **K–B2;** *3* **K–Q7, K–B3;** *4* **B–B4.** The flight via K4 is prevented. *4* . . . , **K–B2;** *5* **B–K5, K–B1;** *6* **K–K6, K–K1;** *7* **B–B7.** The Black K must be driven into the corner

KR8 dominated by the B. *7* . . . , **K–B1;** *8* **Kt–B5, K–K1;** *9* **Kt–Kt7** *ch,* **K–B1;** *10* **K–B6, K–Kt1;** *11* **K–Kt6, K–B1;** *12* **B–Q6** *ch,* **K–Kt1;** *13* **Kt–B5, K–R1;** *14* **B–R3, K–Kt1;** *15* **Kt–R6** *ch,* **K–R1;** *16* **B– QKt2 mate.**

The pawn, itself weak in effect, gains tremendously in power by advancing to the eighth rank where it is promoted to a piece of its own colour. King and Pawn in conjunction can deprive the adverse King of its mobility but they cannot mate him.

Black is Stalemate

Upon promotion the lowly P can become the powerful Q and then decides the combat by a few strokes.

Pawns are frequently blocked by pieces or other pawns, or if not actually blocked they are debarred from advancing by the menace of a hostile pawn on an adjoining file. A pawn free from the embarrassments caused by adverse pawns is called "passed." A passed pawn must be captured by pieces, or blocked, or else it will eventually be promoted. To keep a piece of the opponent engaged to watch it so as somehow to prevent its advance is the effect of a passed pawn. Supposing all the opponent's men to have been captured, the passed pawn exerts its pressure against the adverse King.

The K cannot fulfil its function of capturing or blocking the passed pawn unless in its proximity.

Black, to play, stops the Pawn
White, to play, advances and thereafter queens the P

If the K succeeds in reaching the file of the pawn in time the P will need the support of his K in order to fight against the adverse K. It is then advantageous for the pawn to have his own K in front because the powerful opponent is best combated by an equally powerful ally. Hence in the following position White wins.

White or Black to play. White wins

If White to play, the game takes the course: *1* **K–B6, K–B1;** *2* **P–Kt6, K–Kt1;** *3* **P–Kt7,** Black is now in *"Zugzwang"* **K–R2.** *4* **K–B7.** The K thus guards the square Kt8 and queens the pawn in safety. If Black were to play, White wins more quickly still: *1* . . . **K–B1;** *2* **K–R7,** and the pawn advances now irresistibly.

But the following position leads to a stalemate and therefore to a draw.

White or Black to play. Black draws

1 **K–B6, K–B1;** *2* **P–K7** *ch,* **K–K1.** Now White must move the King. If he goes to K6 Black is stalemate; if he moves elsewhere Black captures the pawn.

The power of the "passed pawn" in an ending may be illustrated in a large variety of ways. Here are a few instances.

White to play and win

White wins by advancing his P, the Black K is thereby forced away from the scene of action. Although he can capture the passed pawn, this cannot prevent disaster on the right wing, where the White K captures the two Black pawns and Queens his remaining P.

White fights the Black R by R–B8. Whether the Black R takes the White R or refuses to capture, the White P will queen.

The following exercises are useful:
WHITE: **K** on **KR6**, **P** on **KR5**; BLACK: **K** on **KR1**. White cannot win, the game ends in a stalemate. Add a White B on KB1 to the White force, the Black K will still be able to hold the KR square and will therefore prevent the White P from queening, and thus draw, but with a White Kt on any indifferent square, say KB1, or a B which can command the Queening square, White will be able to drive the Black K out of the corner and win.

WHITE: **K** on **KB5**, **P** on **Q5**; BLACK: **K** on **KB2**, **P** on **Q3**. White with the move can only draw. Black with the move is under "*Zugzwang*," i.e., forced to abandon the opposition and finally loses. *1* . . . , **K–K2**; *2* **K–Kt6, K–K1**; *3* **K–B6, K–Q2**; *4* **K–B7**, "*Zugzwang*" again! Black at last loses his QP.

The reader should experiment with similar game endings of his own invention.

THE EFFECT OF THE MEN

After having investigated, by logical processes, those fairly simple positions which constitute the elements of the End Game, we now turn to procedures which rely not on logic but on judgment. Our first task is to obtain an insight into the effect of the men. What power have the pieces to aid in the execution of a well conceived plan?

1. The effect of the men is manifold, they give check, they capture pieces, they obstruct hostile forces, thus guarding their King and each other. They restrict the hostile King in his mobility, and thus aid in a checkmate. The player should therefore try to obtain a fairly accurate estimate of what he might expect his pieces to do on the average, and of how much work he might hope to get out of them when at their best. If he knows little of the game his knowledge of these values will be small and as he advances in skill and experience his knowledge of these values will extend, but no matter how much or how little he may know of chess the method of trying in some way to fix these values is serviceable. It is a good method for the master and the tyro alike, and it is applicable to any game and by any one.

2. To begin with the weakest man, the Pawn. As long as it is not promoted it can, at its best, assail two pieces at once, the resulting figure picturesquely is called a "fork."

The White Pawn advances to Kt6 and forks the two Black Rooks, which have difficulty in extricating themselves from their peril.

3. A Kt may at one and the same time assail many pieces, since the range of its mobility may extend to eight squares, but it will do very well if it attacks two heavily armed hostile men simultaneously, as in this further example of "the fork."

The White Kt by capturing the QBP gives check and menaces the Black R at the same time.

4. The B not only can attack several men at the same time but has also the peculiar capacity of "pinning" one of the enemy's men.

The White B moves to Q5 where he is supported by the White Pawn. If Q captures B the P recaptures. The Q is unable to make any different move, because the Black K must not be exposed.

The Black Rook is pinned. Whatever Black moves he cannot avoid losing his Castle. For instance, *1 . . . , B–K3; 2 K–Kt5,* any move; *3 B x R.*

A double attack by the B is all the stronger if the K is involved.

The B goes to Kt2 ch and wins the Q

The white B moves to B4 ch and wins **the R**

5. A Castle also can pin adverse men.

White is in check. He moves R–K2, thus obstructing the Queen and subjecting it to a partial pin, in consequence of which she has to submit to the attack of the R.

White plays B x B. The Black Kt cannot recapture
because he is pinned by the R.

The R also can win pieces by checking.

White by playing R–R8 *ch* wins the Q
and the game.

6. The R and still more so the Q are able to attack two or more pieces at the same time.

The Q wins the R by Q–Kt8 *ch.*

Black to play either moves the K: *1* . . . , **K–KB8;** *2* **Q–KR3** wins, or else moves the R away from the protection of his K and exposes it to danger. *1* . . . , **R–QR7;** *2* **Q–Kt5** *ch*, **K–R8;** *3* **Q–R6** *ch*, **K–Kt8;** *4* **Q–Kt6** *ch*, **K–R7;** *5* **Q–R7** *ch*, **K–Kt8;** *6* **Q–Kt8** *ch* wins the R.

The White Rooks having been doubled on the seventh rank, attack all the Black pawns. They also threaten to checkmate in three moves. How? At the very least Black loses all of his Pawns: *1 . . . ,* **R–B3;** *2* **R x P** *ch,* **K–B1;** *3* **R x RP, K–K1;** *4* **R x P.**

7. The K has considerable sphere of action, an example of a double attack by the K was given above (see the *End Game*). The main function of the K however, is to seek security, because he otherwise serves as a target for ambitious or desperate enemy pieces.

It is fairly easy to checkmate a King who has been inadvertently abandoned by his men, provided the assailant has a very strong piece or two supported by minor pieces at his disposal, for the purpose. But considerably more difficulty is experienced when the King is protected by Pawns.

Black to play, mates quickly, and also if it is White's move it is too late to save the K. Say White plays

1 **R–Kt2, Q–B6;** 2 **R–Kt2, Q–K6** *ch;* 3 **K–R1,
R–R1** *ch;* 4 **R–R2, Q–B6** *ch;* 5 **K–Kt1, R–Kt1** *ch;*
6 **R–Kt2, Q x R** *mate.* Or again: 2 **Q–K1, R–Kt1** *ch;*
3 **K–R2, R–R1** *ch;* 4 **K–Kt1, R–R8** *mate.*

White to play

Black would win by force of numbers if his K were
sufficiently protected. As it is White mates in two
moves:

1 **R– Q8** *ch*	**K–R2**	1	**K–B2**
2 **R–KR8** mates, or		2 **R–KB8** mates.	

Black thinks that the Kt cannot escape because if moved it exposes the R to capture, but it is not so, a check intervenes: *1* **Kt–B6** *ch*, **P x Kt**; *2* **R x R** *ch* and wins.

The variety of attacks against the K is exceedingly large. The student should acquaint himself with a few instances and experiment with them. Here are a few simple exercises that I should recommend:

WHITE: **K on KKt2, R on K1, Kt on KB3, P on K5;** BLACK: **K on KR2, R on KB3, B on Q3, Ps on KKt2 and KR3.**
Black, to play, saves his pieces threatened by the fork.

WHITE: **K on KKt1, Q on QR7, Kt on K4, Ps on QB2, Q3 and KKt2;** BLACK: **K on K1, Q on KB3, R on Q3, P on KB2.**
Black, to play, saves his Queen and R assailed by the Kt.

WHITE: **K** on **QB1**, **Rs** on **QR7** and **QKt7**;
BLACK: **K** on **K1**, **Q** on **QB1**, **P** on **QB6**.

White, to play, wins by R–KR7, threatening mate.

WHITE: **K** on **KB1**, **Q** on **KB6**, **R** on **Q2**, **P** on **KR6**;
BLACK: **K** on **KKt1**, **Q** on **Q1**, **R** on **K2**, **Ps** on **KB2**, **KKt3** and **KR2**.

Black, to play, wins by R–K8 *ch*.

WHITE: **K** on **KKt1**, **Q** on **QR7**, **R** on **K1**, **Kt** on **K4**;
BLACK: **K** on **K1**, **Q** on **Q5**, **Rs** on **Q3** and **Q1**, **B** on **KB1**.

White, to play, wins. By what move?

WHITE: **K** on **KKt1**, **Q** on **QKt8**, **Kt** on **QKt5**, **Ps** on **KB2**, **KKt3**, **KR2**;
BLACK: **K** on **KB2**, **Q** on **KB6**, **B** on **KR6**, **Ps** on **Q3** and **KKt2**.

White, to play, wins by Q–Kt7 *ch*. Why?

♜ ♞ ♝ ♛ X ♚ ♝ ♞ ♜

....

THE START OF THE GAME

AT THE start of the game, the combinations are a long way off. At this stage the pieces are placed in a position of small effect. They obstruct each other. How then should the player guide himself at the start?

The question itself points to its answer. He should guide himself by his sense of the appropriate, which tells him that the pieces should overcome the obstructions which they occasion to each other. Only in this manner will they be enabled to move freely and to seek a target for their activity and to engage the hostile force.

This consideration applies to either player, in fact they are in an equal position, therefore equally obstructed and under the same necessities. The task at the start for the two players, if the comparison may be ventured, is the same as that of two horses at the start of a short race. The horses have to get ready for their gallop, and that side which succeeds in the shorter time has the advantage. Looking at it from this point of view it is easily seen that the most obstructive pieces should be moved out of the way first

of all, and that this principle should be followed again
and again.

The process of getting rid of obstruction indicates
the task of "development." That task requires also
that the men direct their power against vulnerable
targets.

To sum up: At the start of the game the players, by
seeking to get rid of the obstructions which their pieces
cause to each other and to direct their men against
vulnerable targets, should develop their forces at as
rapid a pace as possible.

"Developed Force"? This phrase might be ques-
tioned because it may be misunderstood—The Queen
represents a strong force, yet to send her forth into
the front of the battle would in all likelihood expose
her to danger, since the Q besides being a force is also
a very suitable target for the opponent.

At this point the player is thrown upon his own
judgment. For the usefulness of chess this fact is salu-
tary. A game that does not call forth the initiative and
ingenuity of the player is useless. It is the function of a
good game to make the player rely upon himself and
have belief in himself. As far as logic leads him let him
follow with respect but where logic ceases to lead him
let his judgment be allowed free play.

A careful survey of the initial position discloses that
the KP, the QP, the two Kts and the KB cause most
obstruction to their fellows. These men should be
moved in the opening of the game as soon as the engagement with hostile forces will permit. The proviso
that the opportunity for gaining some other advantage

should not be missed has to be added, but such an opportunity, if it offer itself at all, is rare, since in the first five or six moves the centre of the board is almost empty and therefore presents few targets.

On the theory of the opening many books have been written, some of large volume. What they contain may almost be summed up by what has already been stated. For the guidance of the student a few examples will therefore suffice, and he should rely for further progress rather on his own invention than on compilations, because to train and to improve his judgment is a more important task to him than to store his memory with facts, however valuable as facts they may be, in the field of chess.

1 **P–K4.** This move gets an obstruction to Q, KB, KKt and K out of the way and takes hold of the two central points, Q5 and KB5.

1 . . . , **P–K4.** Black replies in the same way for the same reasons.

2 **Kt–KB3.** The Kt that has obstructed the KR moves towards the centre. It has there a large circle of activity. It acts on the points Q4, K5, KKt5, KR4, and also on points situated in the White camp: Q2, K1, KKt1, KR2, and assails a Black weakness—the K pawn.

2 . . . , **Kt–QB3.** A developing move on the Q side which defends the KP.

3 **B–B4.** The B gets out of the way of K and R, takes up a central position and points towards KB7, which is defended only by the Black K.

3 . . . , **B–B4.** [The "Giuoco Piano" has arisen,

an opening which was most in use in Italy during the time before Castling was introduced.]

4 P–QB3. An attack which has to be carefully met. Its object is to advance with pawns in the centre.

4 . . . , Kt–KB3. Black uses the breathing spell for further development.

5 P–Q4, assailing both B and KP. This P is thrice attacked and thrice defended.

5 . . . , P x P.

6 P x P, B–Kt5 *ch.* Black must not lose time by retreating, hence this check.

7 B– Q2.

7 Kt–B3 might be played with the consequence: 7 . . . , Kt x KP; *8* Castles, unpinning the QKt; *8 . . . ,* Kt x Kt; *9* P x Kt, P–Q4, counter-attacking the B. Of course, many other lines of play are here possible, which the student might try over the board.

7 . . . , B x B *ch.*

8 QKt x B, P–Q4! Black breaks the White centre and thus assures himself of the point Q4, which he manages to maintain.

9 P x P, KKt x P.

10 Q–Kt3, QKt–K2. Also Kt–R4 is possible but it rather misplaces the Kt.

11 O–O, O–O. Neither K wants to stay on the open K line.

12 R–K1. The R is now very active.

12 . . . , P–QB3. Now the position of the Kt on Q4 is unassailable, and the Q gets an outlet to QB2 or QKt3.

Again:

1 **P–K4, P–K4.**

2 **Kt–KB3, Kt–QB3.**

3 **B–Kt5.** [The "Ruy Lopez" named after a Spanish Bishop of the 16th Century.]

3 **. . . , Kt–KB3.** Counter-attack against the White KP.

4 **O–O, P–Q3.** Also *4* Kt x P may be played but leads to complications which a beginner is unlikely to master until after extended trials.

5 **P–Q4, B–Q2.** White threatens P–Q5. Black therefore unpins the Kt.

6 **Kt–B3, B–K2.**

7 **R–K1, P x P.**

8 **Kt x P, O–O.** In this position Black can hold his own, though White dominates more space.

Another defence to the Ruy Lopez: *3* **. . . , P–QR3.** This move dares White to capture the Kt. No material loss would, however, result from *4* B x Kt, QP x B; *5* Kt x P, for Q–Q5 immediately regains the P. *4* **B–R4, Kt–B3;** *5* **O–O, Kt x P;** *6* **P–Q4!** Trying to get the obstructions on the K file out of the way, so as to occupy it with the Castle; *6* **. . . , P–QKt4;** *7* **B–Kt3, P–Q4;** *8* **P x P, B–K3;** *9* **P–QB3.** This gives an outlet to the KB which White desires to preserve in order that shortly it may play against the Black K. *9* **. . . , B–K2;** *10* **QKt–Q2, O–O;** *11* **B–B2.** To drive off the Black Kt. *11* **. . . , P–B4.** Black strengthens the position of the Kt and obtains action for his KR.

1 **P–K4, P–K4;** *2* **Kt–KB3, Kt–KB3.** [The "Petroff" Defence named after a Russian master.] *3* **Kt x P, P–Q3;** this developing move is very useful; *4* **Kt–KB3, Kt x P;** *5* **Q–K2, Q–K2;** *6* **P–Q3, Kt–KB3;** *7* **B–Kt5.** White has slightly the best of it, but one may say that much for all sound lines of play in the opening.

1 **P–K4, P–K4;** *2* **P–KB4.** A "Gambit" opening intended to break the even tenor of development. *2* **. . . , P x P.** Black might reply in many ways, for instance *2* . . . , B–B4 or *2* . . . , P–Q4, but to capture the P is also good. *3* **Kt–KB3, P–KKt4.** Black wants to hold on to his material advantage, and is determined to meet the impending attack. *4* **B–B4, B–Kt2;** *5* **P–Q4, P–Q3;** *6* **P–KR4, P–KR3.** The Black KR being guarded, Black may venture on this move. *7* **P–QB3, Kt–QB3.** Black is sufficiently well developed, White cannot easily get the upper hand on any essential point.

The student should try out gambits in over-the-board play with his friends.

1 **P–Q4.** This move also gets an obstruction out of the way and takes hold of two important central points: *1* **. . . , P–Q4;** *2* **P–QB4.** The offer of this gambit involves no sacrifice, since White can easily regain the P or, better still, leave the P a target and develop rapidly. *2* **. . . , P–K3;** *3* **Kt–QB3, KKt–B3;** *4* **Kt–B3, QKt–Q2.** This position is very effective; it contests the points K4 and QB4. The blockade of the QB is only temporary. *5* **B–Kt5, B–K2;** *6* **P–K3, O–O;** *7* **R–QB1, P–QB3;** *8* **B–Q3, P x P;** *9* **B x P, Kt–Q4.** Black thus frees his position. *10* **B x B, Q x B;** *11* **O–O, Kt x Kt;** *12* **R x Kt, P–K4** and Black has liberated his B.

To gain a knowledge of other openings the reader may look over the games of Masters that are discussed at the end of this book. The student in the course of his chess practice will have occasion to become acquainted with many openings. Let him try to follow the principles laid down, unafraid of traps and brilliant coups which occasionally will take him unawares. Critical analysis of his losses will teach him more than books can do. The above few lines of play suffice as an introduction to him who wants to rely mainly upon himself and to develop his own resources.

XI

PRINCIPLES OF CHESS STRATEGY

IN THE opening the forces have marched up to battle array. Then, having got into touch with each other, they come into collision. How is the intelligent player to conduct a campaign that is approaching a crisis? His men, at the start so obstructed, are now rich in mobility. Possibilities for attack and defence abound. How, out of the multitude of possibilities that suggest themselves to him, is he to select the right move—or a move that, according to his standards, is intelligent?

His first consideration should be that his moves, to be intelligent, must carry the mark of intelligence, which is Connection and Plan. A disconnected move is one made uncritically, unreflectingly, and without foresight. It suggests itself probably as being in the nature of a trap, but it is really without force. If the opponent is taken unawares the scheme succeeds, but should the opponent on his part use foresight, the attempt recoils on the schemer.

Here then we have the conception that should mould the plan of the player: *Force*.

Of two groups of men that are ready to engage with each other that one is entitled to gain the upper hand which has the most force behind it. This principle is fundamental. If your experience does not conform to it, not the principle but your application of it is at fault. In that case you have to review your valuation of the forces engaged and be attentive to mistakes. If your valuation was precise, the weaker side cannot gain a lasting success. An apparent success—why not?—but not a lasting success. Such is the nature of force. This principle will guide you in extending and improving your scale of values.

Strange as it may seem, the human mind has taken a long time to learn how to apply the concept of force to chess. The mistake committed was to confound force and effect. Force is composed of two factors: the effect, and the thing susceptible to the effect.

An effect and a target combined make a force. The effect has a magnitude, and the susceptibility of the target has a measure, and the combination of these two elements constitutes the force.

Take as an instance a-Q. A mobile Q is capable of many effects, but if the hostile men are protected even the Q is dependent upon the co-operation of other pieces in order to exert force.

A position, as a rule, contains elements strongly susceptible to effects. The technical term for such an element is a "weak" point, or "weakness." Thus the position of the K is weak when aggressors find few obstructions in the K's quarter, and a player discerns a "weak point" in the opponent's camp when he sees that the opponent cannot assail a piece placed on that point. If that point is occupied by a man which from there exerts strong force the player has occupied a "strong point."

Weakness may be mobile or stationary. *A concentration of effect on a weakness will pay only if that weakness is stationary*, for otherwise, by simply the shifting of the weakness, the concentrated effect would hit an empty spot and therefore be wasted. Stationary weaknesses are, a King who can no longer castle and is defended by relatively few pieces, or to whom access is easy; a pinned piece, a piece of little mobility—e.g., one which has been shut in, or whose movement would entail heavy loss, or, a frequent case, a blocked pawn.

Let us first of all survey a few instances:

The Black R on Kt2 being pinned is a target calling for concentration of effect of the White pieces. *1* Q–K7, White wishes to eliminate, to exchange the Black Q which not only would defend but threaten counter attacks at the same time. *1* . . . , Q x Q. (Not so good would be *1* . . . , Q–KKt1; *2* Q x P, R–QB1; *3* B x R *ch* wins). *2* R x Q, R–KKt1; *3* R x P,

P–Kt3; *4* R x P, P–R3; *5* R–Kt7, K–R2; *6* B x R.
The R has to be captured since it threatened to become mobile. *6* . . . , R x B; *7* R x P or R x R and
wins by superiority of material force.

The Kt must not move on penalty of abandoning
the B which he protects. It is therefore the indicated
target. *7* R–K5 wins B or Kt.

The King has to guard the Q, has therefore little
mobility and is a welcome object of attack. *7* R–K8 *ch*
wins Q for R.

White espies a target: the QRP, which, being un-able to receive support from a pawn, handicaps the Black pieces that have to support it. *1* R–R6, which binds the B to its post. Now the target is immobile. *1* . . . , K–Q1; *2* KR–R1, and now the target is over-whelmed; *2* . . . , K–B1; *3* R x P, R x R; *4* R x R, K–Kt1; *5* R–R1. White has won a pawn and therefore enters upon the ending with a considerable advantage.

Black's K side is weak because the White Bishops bear down upon it. But White must hurry, for Black

contemplates the obstruction of one of the Bishops by
P–KB4. White conceives a plan by which to expose
the Black K, then to limit its range, and finally to
assault it decisively. *1* B x P *ch*, K x B; *2* Q x Kt *ch*,
K–Kt1; *3* B x P, K x B. The K is now badly exposed.
4 Q–Kt4 *ch*, K–R2 (if K–B3; *5* Q–Kt5 mates). Now
the K has little mobility. *5* R–B3. The decisive R–R3
cannot be forestalled. *5* . . . , P–K4. To allay the
fierce onslaught by the sacrifice of the Q; *6* R–R3 *ch*,
Q–R3; *7* R x Q *ch*, K x R; *8* Q–Q7 wins another
piece and the game:

The analyst examines *all* points of the board to
ascertain upon which side is the superior force. Each
side has the advantage in its own camp. The point
Q5—Black's Q4—is hotly contested. The White QR
will be sooner developed that the Black QR, consequently White is stronger than Black on the QB file.
Also on the central points K4, K5, QB5. Black cannot
keep the balance and must eventually give ground.

Black to play

The Black Kt is momentarily in a weak position, but can take up a safe and strong post on K2. The Black QBP cannot be protected by pawns and if assailed by White Rooks is therefore a handicap on some of the Black pieces. It will pay to experiment with this position—*1* . . . , P–KB3, to get the R into action; *2* R–B1, Q–Q2; *3* Q–B2, and wins the QBP. Again: *1* . . . , Kt–R4; *2* R–B1, Kt–B5; *3* P–QKt3, Kt–Kt3; *4* R–B6, Q–Q2; *5* Q–B2, R–R2; *6* R–B1, Kt–R1; *7* Q–B5, Kt–Kt3; *8* P–KR3. White must not take the BP at once (*8* R x BP? R x R; *9* Q x R, R–QB1 wins) but the P remains weak and is certain to fall in the end.

Fleeting, or temporary weaknesses, such as a mobile but unprotected man, or a piece of high value on a point easily accessible, may also be taken advantage of, but by a process that wholly differs from that to be followed against a more permanent weakness due to lack of mobility. To attack a transitory weakness merely to make the power of one's pieces manifest is bad play. The attack is useful only when with the same move some other advantage is gained. For instance, when an attack on several mobile weaknesses is simultaneously instituted. The defender then has the hard task of extricating himself from several perils, and has only one move to do this with. A task solvable only by counter attack against some momentary weakness of his assailant.

White attacks the transitory weakness KB6, he has himself a temporary weakness on QB4. Black, instead of withdrawing the Kt counter-attacks with P–Q4! The threat to capture the B is meant as compensation for White's threat to capture the Kt. A solid and permanent advantage is thereby gained by Black on the score of his development.

What does the term "overwhelm" imply? Under what conditions is a weakness overwhelmed? The rule that applies thereto is simple. When the pieces captured on a point represent higher value than the pieces lost in the struggle on that point, the assailant achieves an advantage on that point. Most frequently the *number* of pieces captured is the measure, but by no means always. If the K is checkmated the assailant may sacrifice any number of pieces to that end and still be the gainer, and a Q and sometimes a Rook are of so high a value that their gain is sufficient compensation for the loss of several men. If the pieces involved in attack and defence are of equal value, the player must count the number of threats directed against a point and compare it with the number of protections—i.e., of men ready to recapture on that point—in order to decide whether the attack against the point has succeeded in gaining the upper hand or not. Even if the attack will achieve that measure of success it does not follow that to bring it home at once would be the right play. The assailant may bring additional force to bear on the immobile weakness and be a gainer thereby, but he must not strike while he maintains this advantage. Consequently he must consider whether the reserve force which he can bring to bear upon the weakness is as great or greater than the reserve force which the defender can bring up in the same time.

The conception of value is therefore bound up with that of force, which again implies those of effect and weakness. You may change the rules of chess, enlarge the board, increase the number of men, vary their mobility, do all this to any extent and yet the above reasoning will apply. This consideration shows that in the above conceptions we have in hand something which is useful beyond the narrow limits of chess.

How to value things is a problem of exceeding importance. In life we have to judge men, actions, chances and risks, services and sacrifices, and this is a responsible task. By what standards is just valuation guided?

The ordinary standard is that of utility, but one has to be wary in its application. In the position White K on KR6, P on KKt7, Black K on KR1, B on KKt1, Q on KB4. The pawn checkmates and is therefore more useful to White than the Q and the B are to Black. Yet a Pawn is very much weaker than Queen or Bishop. Possibly Black in allowing this situation to arise has committed a grievous blunder, or else it has been brought about by White's sacrifice of powerful pieces—for instance, the P had been on KB6, a White Q on KB8, a Black R on KKt8, White had played Q–KKt7 *ch*, and thus by the sacrifice of the Q forced the mate by the pawn. We have to distinguish between temporary and permanent values, and we have to exclude blunders.

The permanent value of a group of men is the measure of its utility in the hands of the master under varying conditions. Temporary value of a group of men in a certain situation is the measure of its utility under given conditions, again provided that the play is conducted by a master. If we follow the games of a master who contends against an opponent of his own mettle we may keep an account of the force of each of his pieces as it is shown in the course of his games and thus gain a reliable measure for the permanent value of each of the pieces. Since absolute perfection does not exist, this method can be executed only with such approximation to truth as is accorded by substituting a very strong player for the ideal perfect master. The judgment of the master has authority. The written and printed word of the master should be consulted. Thus we can supplement our own endeavour by taking advice from Authority and Tradition. Nevertheless we should not attain our end by relying wholly on Authority and Tradition. The judgment of a man is the fountain out of which springs his thoughts and progress. If he abandons his judgment in favour of Authority he ceases to be original. In that case he is bound to commit mistakes, because he needs judgment to understand the master. If on the other hand he stoutly maintains his right to use his own judgment he keeps the springs of his creative thought alive and is one of those privileged to help along progress.

I therefore advise my pupils to be critical of valuations imposed upon them by others, and to be diligent in attempting to arrive at valuations by their own efforts.

A table of simplest values in chess—that of the men themselves—was devised long ago. Leonhard Euler, the mathematician, showed the way to calculate these values mathematically by the principle that the average utility of a man is proportionate to its average mobility. This assumption is correct, because according to the rules of chess the effect of a man on a point is 0 when the man cannot move to the point, and is 1 for any man which can move to the point. This reasoning does not apply to the promotion of a Pawn. The Pawn therefore gains in value at the End Game stage. Apart from this factor, Leonhard Euler's method is sound, and the values he thus found agreed with those based on experience. The following table indicates the approximately correct valuation of the pieces:

$$Kt = 3 \text{ Ps;} \quad B = Kt; \quad R = Kt + 2 \text{ Ps.}$$

$$Q = 2 \text{ Rs} = 3 \text{ Kts;} \quad K = Kt + P,$$

But this table is only the beginning of the work of valuation. Whenever a player is meditating upon abandoning some values in order to gain a compensating advantage he has to compare what he intends to give up with what he hopes to gain. If he lacks the capacity for independent and fearless valuation he cannot do justice to positions of this kind.

A frequently occurring instance is the sacrifice of a pawn for advantages gained in development. What advantage in development maintains the balance for the loss of a pawn? Perhaps no master has ever been able to give a fully satisfying answer to this question, though a good deal of Chess Strategy depends upon it. The player of natural talent answers the question by weighing the issues of the position and letting his judgment decide.

A good method for creating and training a sound judgment is to experiment with advantages and compensations so as to produce a balance. Let a player, for instance, endeavour to find out which of the two minor pieces, Kt and B, is in a given case the stronger or more valuable piece. To that end, according to the experimental method above alluded to, he will set up a balanced position—say of K, 5P and a Rook each, with nearly equal weaknesses—and he will then add a Kt to the one side, a B to the other, and see by analysis, or at least by a series of trials, which side gets the advantage. If he varies the balanced position in material and weaknesses the continued exercise will at length develop his judgment for the distinction between Kt and B to a fine point. Let the student begin with simple tasks of this kind before he attacks the more complicated ones. I indicate here a few instances:

WHITE: K on **QR1**, Kt on **QB3**, P on **QR5**.
BLACK: K on **KR1**, B on **K3**, P on **KR5**.
White to play. *1* P–R6, B–B1; *2* P–R7, B–Kt2; *3* Kt–Q1, P–R6; *4* Kt–B2, P–R7. Black has the advantage. Add a couple of safe pawns say White on QB2, and Black on KB2, and Black wins easily. Thus, if the weaknesses of White and Black are very far apart the B is stronger than the Kt.

WHITE: K on **QR1**, Kt on **QB3**, P on **QKt4**.
BLACK: K on **QKt1**, B on **K3**, P on **QB5**.
White to play. *1* K–Kt2, K–B2; *2* K–B1, K–Q3; *3* K–Q2, K–K4; *4* K–K3.
White has the advantage, which would be very pronounced if his K had been able to gain the point —K4. Add two pawns, White on KB2, Black on KB2, and White will probably win. If the weaknesses on

either side are in proximity, the Kt is stronger than the B.

WHITE: **K** on **Q3**, **B** on **KB7**.

BLACK: **K** on **QKt4**, **B** on **KB3**, **Ps** on **QB4**, **QKt5**, **QR6**.

Black cannot force the win. *1* . . . , K–R5; *2* K–B2 P–Kt6 *ch*; *3* B x P *ch*, K–Kt5. Black goes the only possible way of advancing some of his pawns on to White squares. *4* B–R2, P–B5; *5* B–Kt1. And that way also leads to a draw. Consequently the B supports the advance of its pawns best when they are on points of a colour differing from those of the points it dominates. The other way—leaving the pawns on points dominated by the B—is the right way for defence, but it is the wrong way for attack.

WHITE: **K** on **KR5**, **R** on **QKt1**.

BLACK: **K** on **KKt1**, **R** on **QR3**, **Ps** on **QR2** and **KR3**.

White to play. *1* R–Kt7, K–B1; *2* R–KR7, K–K1; *3* K–Kt4, K–Q1; *4* K–B3, K–B1; *5* R–R8 *ch*, K–Kt2; *6* R–R7 *ch*. Black cannot win. The position of the White Rook on KR7 where it exerts force on two weak Black pawns, is so strong that it leaves his K free to select the quarter where it is required to fight.

WHITE: **K** on **K3**, **B** on **Q5**, **Kt** on **K4**, **P** on **QB4**.

BLACK: **K** on **KKt3**, **Q** on **Q1**, **P** on **K4**.

White has a firm position, the only object for attack is the K, provided the White pieces are careful to retain their strong posts. For the attack against the K Black has K, Q, and to a slight extent the blocked P at his disposal. Black's plan will be to attain a position where the White K is driven back and the Black K has advanced to KB5, with say, White K on K2, and Black Q on QKt6. The continuation might be: *1* . . . , Q–K6 *ch*; *2* K–Q1, Q–Q6 *ch*; *3* K–B1, K–K6; *4* K–Kt2, K–Q5; *5* K–B1. Now White hardly dares to move any piece but the King. It is, therefore, advisable to employ *Zugzwang*. *5* . . . , Q–KB6; *6* K–B2, Q–K6; *7* K–Kt2, Q–Q6, and now if *8* K–R2, Q–B7 *ch*; *9* K–R3, Q–Kt8; *10* K–R4, Q–Kt3; *11* K–R3, K–Q6. Will Black be able to win? There are many lines of play. Some of the essential ones have not been mentioned above. The student will do well to try them out for himself—after using the method of imagining a hoped-for position and aiming for it. The preponderance of the Q over the White pieces, firmly posted though they are, and the nature of the advantage she holds is, for the rest, quite clear.

Let me insist again that the individual result is of far less importance than the acquisition of ease in handling the method. Chess is an occasion to judge the method, its field of application is as wide as life itself.

The conception of "Balance" often called (according to the great Chess thinker and Master, William Steinitz) "Balance of position" is more fundamental than it would appear above. Chess is really not embracing enough to give full sway and scope to that conception. The conception of Balance functions in the whole of social life. The values that are essential to chess, though manifold, are not so nicely graded as to form a continuous series, therefore a perfectly balanced position does not exist in chess. In a symmetrical position the move would make a difference, though in practice that might amount to very little, and the game therefore might easily end in a draw. All the same the position would not correspond to the conditions of a perfect balance.

Let us for the moment forget that we study chess and let us envisage what the conception of Balance, purely as a conception entails:

1. In a balanced position neither side is able to gain an advantage by force.

2. In a balanced position, any attempt to win an advantage however well planned, can be frustrated. And we may be permitted to add:

3. In a nearly balanced position any attack, however profoundly conceived, intended to obtain a considerable advantage, can be repulsed and recoils to the disadvantage of the assailant if the defender succeeds in doing full justice to the resources at his command.

[N.B. The difficulty in any abstract reasoning on Chess is mainly its lack of grading in the final result. Loss. Draw. Win. This is the scale of success in Chess. Life is infinitely more varied. Life goes on, it knows no permanent defeat, nor permanent victory, therefore one cannot detect in Chess such striking and exact application of the concepts of Force, Value, Balance as can be found in life.]

Now the conception of an "Approximate Balance" may be used in chess, even by the most conscientious and exacting. The greater force will gain the greater advantage—that hardly needs a demonstration in Euclidean style.

Let us give a few instances of how the principles set forth function in Chess:

WHITE: **K** on **KKt3**, **R** on **QR3**, **P** on **KB4**.
BLACK: **K** on **KKt3**, **R** on **QKt3**, **P** on **KB4**.

He who tries to win gets the worst of it. *1* K–R4, R to QB3; *2* R–Kt3 *ch*, K–B3; *3* K–R5, R–B8; *4* R–Kt6 *ch*, K–B2; *5* R–QR6, R–KKt8. The game is drawn, but White has to play carefully.

In the initial position after *1* **P–K4, P–K4;** *2* **Kt–KB3, Kt–QB3;** *3* **B–B4, B–B4;** *4* **P–Q3, P–Q3,** White now attacks *5* **Kt–Kt5.** This move discloses an attempt to win, which, in the balanced position, is unjustified; *5* . . . , **Kt–R3;** *6* **Q–R5, O–O;** *7* **Kt–QB3, Kt–Q5.** Black makes a counter attack, White is in difficulties.

Again the initial position *1* **P–K4, P–K4;** *2* **Kt–KB3, Kt–QB3;** *3* **B–Kt5, P–KB4.** An unjustifiable attack. *4* **Kt–QB3, P x P;** *5* **QKt x P, P–Q4;** *6* **Kt–Kt3, P–K5;** *7* **Kt–K5, Q–B3;** *8* **P–Q4.** Black's attempt has failed.

Again; *1* **P–K4, P–K4;** *2* **Kt–KB3, Kt–QB3;** *3* **P–B3,** an ambitious move, that is not called for, White wants to dominate the central points by pawns *3*

. . . **P–Q4**; *4* **B–Kt5, P x P**; *5* **Kt x P, Q–Q4**; *6* **Q–R4, Kt–K2**; *7* **P–KB4.** Apparently a bad position for Black, since White menaces B–B4. But it cannot be—Black has not transgressed—Black *must* have a sound defence—search! *7* . . . **B–Q2!** This turns the tables on White. *8* **Kt x B, K x Kt.** To give an instance of the possibilities of this position: *9* **O–O, Kt–B4**; *10* **P–QKt4, P–QR4**; *11* **K–R1, P x P**; *12* **B x Kt** *ch*, **P x B**; *13* **Q x R, B–B4**; *14* **Q x R, Kt–Kt6** *ch*; *15* **P x Kt, Q–R4,** mates. An actual game!

From what precedes it is sufficiently clear that three modes of intelligent proceeding may be distinguished in Chess. Firstly Attack, which concentrates effort on one or more weaknesses in the opponent's camp with the intention of forcing the opponent to defend, and finally to gain an advantage thereby. Secondly, Defence, which obstructs the efforts of the enemy, or concentrates efforts on its own weaknesses, or shifts these weaknesses, or makes some sacrifice of material to allay the fury of the onslaught. Thirdly, Development, which does not concentrate effort, but spreads it, so as to gain in mobility, in readiness to attack or to defend. A move that does no good in any one of these ways is indifferent or unintelligible. The main principle of attack is economy of its chances. The attack has to gain the utmost advantage of which it is capable. To win a lesser advantage than should accrue from the position is the mark of an assailant of mediocre ability.

The main principle of Defence is economy of its

risks. The defence must make the smallest sacrifice that suffices to end the attack. To concede a greater advantage than is needed is the mark of a defender of mediocre ability.

The main principle of Development is economy of time. The Development should be as rapid as possible, so that the state of readiness should be reached after as few moves as possible. Loose handling of this principle marks a player who is without ambition to impose responsibilities upon himself.

This sums up the working in Chess of the principle of Economy, that in philosophical language of the Middle Ages was expressed as follows:—"Natura non agit frustra."

I should like to feel that I have made my readers eager to follow this principle according to their standard, high or low, on good days and bad. They will certainly lose many games by attempting it, but if they bear their misfortune in good humour and are attentive in analysing their failures, and succeed in pinning down their mistakes they will in the end rise above mediocrity, and their style of play will have some of the charm of Art.

The above considerations are applicable to all board games and to much else. The method implied by them deserves to be widely known. I call it the method of values.

XII

EXAMPLES OF THE PLAY OF MASTERS
WITH EXPLANATORY NOTES

THE FRENCH DEFENCE

WHITE: *Fritz*　　BLACK: *Mason*

1 P–K4	P–K3

Black develops without exposing his KP.

2 P–Q4	P–Q4
3 Kt–QB3	Kt–KB3
4 B–Kt5	B–K2
5 B x Kt	B x B
6 Kt–B3	O–O
7 P–K5	B–K2
8 B–Q3	P–QKt3

This is too slow. Better to engage White immediately by *8* . . . P–QB4.

9 P–KR4	. . . .

Intending an attack against the Black King.

9	B–Kt2

Far too slow. At least *9* . . . B–R3 should be played.

10 B x P *ch*	K x B
11 Kt–Kt5 *ch*	K–Kt3

If *11 . . .* , K–Kt1; *12* Q–R5 or if *11 . . .* , K–R3; *12* Q–Q2.

12	Kt–K2	**B x Kt**
13	**P x B**	**P–KB4**
14	**KtP x P** e.p.	**R–R1**
15	**Kt–B4** *ch*	**K–B2**
16	**Q–Kt4**	**R x R** *ch*
17	**K–Q2**	**P x P**
18	**Q x P** *ch*	**K–Kt2**
19	**R x R**	**B–B1**
20	**R–R7** *ch*	**K x R**
21	**Q–B7** *ch*	

and mates next move.

KING'S PAWN OPENING

WHITE: *Charousek*   BLACK: *Burn*

1	**P–K4**	**P–K4**
2	**P–KB4**	**P x P**
3	**Kt–KB3**	**P–KKt4**
4	**P–KR4**	**P–Kt5**
5	**Kt–K5**	**B–Kt2**
6	**P–Q4**	**Kt–KB3**
7	**Kt x KtP**	**Kt x P**
8	**B x P**	**Q–K2**
9	**Q–K2**	**B x P**

Had Black played for development, *9 . . .* P–Q4 would have been the move.

10	**P–B3**	**B–Kt2**
11	**Kt–K3**	**Q–K3**
12	**P–KKt3**	**O–O**
13	**B–R3**	**P–KB4**

14	O–O	P–Q3
15	Kt–Q2	Kt x Kt
16	Q x Kt	Kt–B3
17	QR–K1	Q–B2
18	B–Kt2	K–R1
19	Kt–Q5	Kt–K4
20	B–Kt5	P–B3

Black should develop by B–K3 and QR–K1.

21	Kt–B4	P–Q4?
22	P–R5	B–Q2

Now that the Kt on K4 has to be supported by the KB, Black cannot play P–KR 3 on account of B x P.

23	P–R6	B–B3
24	B x B *ch*	Q x B
25	Kt–R5	Q–Q3
26	R x Kt	Q x R
27	R–K1	. . . .

The Queen can no longer guard the point Q5, so Black resigns.

ZUKERTORT'S OPENING

WHITE: *Kevitz*   BLACK: *Alekhin*

1	Kt–KB3	Kt–KB3
2	P–B4	. . . .

A variation favoured by Reti.

2	. . . .	P–QKt3
3	P–KKt3	B–Kt2

Black exerts pressure on K5 so as to impede the advance of the White KP and to gain a foothold in the centre.

4	B–Kt2	P–K4
5	Kt–B3	B–Kt5
6	O–O	B x QKt

To make sure of the point K5.

7	KtP x B	P–Q3
8	P–Q4	. . . .

This move allows Black the mastery over K5. Better was 8 P–Q3.

8	. . . .	P–K5
9	Kt–R4	O–O
10	P–B3	P x P
11	B x P	Kt–K5
12	Q–Q3	R–K1
13	P–Q5	. . . .

This move fixes the White Pawns, and thus changes them from fighting units into mere obstructions and targets. The proper policy is 13 Kt–B5–K3–Q5.

13	. . . .	Kt–B4
14	Q–Q4	QKt–Q2
15	B–R5	Kt–K4

The Black Kts take up positions unassailable by pawns.

16	B–B4	Q–Q2
17	Kt–B3	Kt–Kt3
18	Kt–Q2	Q–R6
19	B x Kt	. . . .

Better was 19 B–B3 for the protection of the K side and to be able to drive the Black Q off.

19	. . . .	RP x B
20	P–K4	P–KB3
21	QR–K1	P–KKt4

These pawns dominate black points. The B on Kt2 will dominate important white points, therefore Black is strong on all essential points.

22	B–K3	R–K2
23	K–R1	QR–K1
24	B–Kt1	B–B1
25	R–B3	B–Kt5
26	KR–K3	Q–R4
27	K–Kt2	B–R6 *ch*
28	K–R1	K–B2

Black prepares the final assault by playing his K over to the safe wing.

29	B–B2	P–R4
30	B–Kt1	R–K4
31	B–B2	Q–Kt5
32	B–Kt1	QR–K2
33	B–B2	K–K1
34	B–Kt1	K–Q1
35	B–B2	K–B1
36	B–Kt1	Q–R4
37	B–B2	B–Kt5
38	K–Kt2	Q–R6 *ch*
39	K–R1	P–R5
40	B–Kt1	P–Kt3

At last the assault begins in earnest.

41	B–B2	K–Kt2
42	B–Kt1	K–R3

Still Black prepares.

43	B–B2	P–B4
44	P x P	P x P
45	R x R	P x R

If now *46* R x P, R x R; *47* Q x R, B–B6 *ch*; *48*
Kt x B, Q–B8 *ch*; *49* Kt–Kt1, Kt–Q6 wins.

46 Q–K3	P–K5
47 P–Q6	. . . .

Trying to confuse the issue.

47	P x P

Black remains calm.

48 Q–Q4	P–B5
49 Resigns	

RUY LOPEZ

WHITE: *Capablanca*   BLACK: *Dr. Bernstein*

1	P–K4	P–K4
2	Kt–KB3	Kt–QB3
3	B–Kt5	Kt–B3
4	O–O	B–K2
5	Kt–B3	P–Q3
6	B x Kt *ch*	. . . .

This is not called for, and rather eases Black's task.

6	. . . .	P x B
7	P–Q4	P x P

Also *7* . . . Kt–Q2 was a good move, since it
maintains the P on K4 and its hold on Q5.

8	Kt x P	B–Q2
9	B–Kt5	O–O
10	R–K1	P–KR3
11	B–R4	Kt–R2
12	B x B	Q x B
13	Q–Q3	QR–Kt1
14	P–QKt3	Kt–Kt4
15	QR–Q1	Q–K4

To forestall White's Q–R6, which would attack two pawns.

16	**Q–K3**	**Kt–K3**
17	**QKt–K2**	**Q–QR4**

Black could very well have exchanged Kt's so as to give free scope to the B. The move of the Q is an adventure in which Black hopes to gain a pawn.

18	**Kt–B5**	**Kt–B4**
19	**Kt(K2)–Q4**	**. . . .**

The White Kt advances in the centre, taking care to occupy points not easily assailable.

19	**. . . .**	**K–R2**
20	**P–KKt4**	**. . . .**

Further to strengthen the position of the Kt on B5, which has a strong effect on many points in the enemy's camp.

20	**. . . .**	**R(Kt1)–K1**
21	**P–KB3**	**Kt–K3**
22	**Kt–K2**	**Q x P**

Black's judgment here is at fault. He should defend by Q–Kt3.

23	**Kt(K2)–Kt3**	**Q x BP**
24	**R–QB1**	**Q–Kt7**
25	**Kt–R5**	**. . . .**

The Black Kt has to guard the KtP, and is therefore pinned to his post, and is a suitable target.

25	**. . . .**	**R–KR1**
26	**R–K2**	**Q–K4**

The Q wants to guard the weak points KKt 2 and KB3.

27	**P–B4**	**Q–Kt4**
28	**Kt(B5) x KtP**	....

If *28* . . . , Kt x Kt; *29* Kt–B6 *ch*, with deadly effect.

28	....	**Kt–B4**

The best move in the unfavourable conditions was R–Q1. White would then continue P–B5 and keep his advantage, but the move in the text is equivalent to resignation without a fight.

29	**Kt x R**	**B x Kt**
30	**Q–QB3**	**P–B3**
31	**Kt x P** *ch*	**K–Kt3**
32	**Kt–R5**	**R–Kt1**
33	**P–B5** *ch*	**K–Kt4**
34	**Q–K3** *ch*	**K–R5**
35	**Q–Kt3** *ch*	Resigns

THE FOUR KNIGHTS OPENING

WHITE: *Bogoljubow*   BLACK: *Grünfeldt*

1	**P–K4**	**P–K4**
2	**Kt–KB3**	**Kt–QB3**
3	**Kt–B3**	**Kt–B3**
4	**B–Kt5**	**B–Kt5**
5	**O–O**	**O–O**
6	**P–Q3**	**B x Kt**
7	**P x B**	**P–Q3**
8	**P–KR3**	....

To avoid the pin B–Kt5, White desires to keep his Kt.

8	....	**P–KR3**

9	R–K1	P–R3
10	B–R4	B–Q2
11	B–Kt3	Kt–QR4

Black is rather too anxious for exchanges. Kt–K2 would suggest itself.

12	Kt–R2	Kt x B
13	RP x Kt	Kt–R2
14	P–KB4	P x P
15	B x P	P–KB4

A mistake. P–KB3 was indicated so as to impede the advance of the KP.

16	P–K5	P x P
17	R x P	Kt–B3
18	Q–K2	R–K1
19	Kt–B3	Kt–Q4
20	B–Q2	Q–B3
21	R–K1	

White holds on to the K file.

21	. . . .	P–B3
22	P–B4	Kt–B2
23	B–B3	Kt–K3

Black defends well, but to no purpose, because White has become too strong.

24	Q–B2	R–KB1
25	Q–Kt6	QR–Kt1
26	R x Kt	Q x B
27	R–K7	B–K1
28	Q–B7	B–R4
29	R(K1)–K5	Resigns

NIMZOWITSCH'S ATTACK

WHITE: *Nimzowitsch*   BLACK: *Roselli*

1 Kt–KB3	P–Q4
2 P–QKt3	P–QB4
3 P–K3	Kt–QB3
4 B–Kt2	B–Kt5
5 P–KR3	B x Kt
6 Q x B	P–K4

Black having given away his QB should guard the White points in his camp by pawns, consequently P–K3 was the right move. To counteract the White B on QKt2 Black could have utilised his B by playing it, say, to K4.

7 B–Kt5	Q–Q3

This ties down the Q. Better would have been 7 . . . P–B3.

8 P–K4	P–Q5

The move Kt–K2 would have been preferable had P–B3 been played. Now White has the superiority on all the white squares.

9 Kt–R3	P–B3
10 Kt–B4	Q–Q2
11 Q–R5 *ch*	P–Kt3
12 Q–B3	. . . .

White desires to weaken the Black KBP.

12	Q–QB2
13 Q–Kt4	. . . .

Threatening Q–K6 *ch*. If *13* . . . Q–B1 then *14* Kt–R5 with evident advantage.

13	**K–B2**
14 **P–B4**	

The position of the Black K is now the target. To begin with, obstructions are got out of the way.

14	**P–KR4**
15 **Q–B3**	**P x P**
16 **B x Kt**	**P x B**

If Q x B then 17 Q x BP R–K1 18 O–O and White should win, as pointed out by Nimzowitsch.

17 **O–O**	**P–Kt4**
18 **P–B3**	**R–Q1**
19 **QR–K1**	**Kt–K2**
20 **P–K5**	

This loosens the chain of Black pawns.

20	**Kt–B4**
21 **P x QP**	**Kt x P**

Or if 21 . . . P x QP; 22 P x P, K x P; 23 Q–K4 with advantage, as shown by Nimzowitsch.

22 **Q–K4**	**B–K2**
23 **P–KR4**	**Q–Q2**
24 **P x BP**	**B x P**
25 **P x P**	Resigns

For if 25 . . . B–Kt2; 26 Kt–K5 *ch*, B x Kt; 27 Q x B and the Black K is in a position which cannot be defended.

MAX LANGE'S ATTACK

WHITE: *Tschigorin*   BLACK: *Teichmann*

1 **P–K4**	**P–K4**
2 **Kt–KB3**	**Kt–QB3**

3 B–B4	B–B4
4 O–O	Kt–B3
5 P–Q4	P x P
6 P–K5	P–Q4

Black replies by counter attack which develops inactive force at the same time.

7 P x Kt	P x B
8 R–K1 *ch*	B–K3
9 Kt–Kt5	Q–Q4

White threatened Kt x B followed by Q–R5 *ch*, which wins the B.

10 Kt–QB3	Q–B4

The QKt must not be taken because the QB is pinned, therefore the Q is unprotected.

11 QKt–K4	B–Kt3

Black hopes to be able to withstand White's attack. The question whether he can do so or not is still undecided.

12 P x P	R–KKt1
13 P–KKt4	Q–Kt3
14 Kt x B	P x Kt
15 B–Kt5	. . . .

This prevents Castling, and commands important points weak in the Black camp. It also obstructs the KKt file.

15	R x P

If *15* . . . P–KR3; *16* Q–B3, P x B ?; *17* Kt–B6 *ch*, K–B2; *18* R x P ! K x R ?; *19* R–K1 *ch* and White wins.

16 Q–B3	P–K4

His position is too insecure, he should sacrifice

something in order to eliminate a White piece *16*
. . . , R–B2; *17* Kt–B6 *ch*, R x Kt; *18* B x R, K–Q2.
The strong Black pawns are a sufficient compensation
for the loss of the exchange.

17 **Kt–B6** *ch*	**K–B2**
18 **P–KR4**	**P–KR3**
19 **Kt–K4** *ch*	**K–K3**
20 **P–R5**	. . . .

To drive the Q from the KKt file and thus to secure
the KKtP.

20	**Q–B2**
21 **B–B6**	. . . .

White's Q is powerful; he, therefore, without question refuses to exchange it.

21	**R(Kt2)–Kt1**
22 **Q–B5** *ch*	**K–Q4**
23 **P–Kt3**	**R x P** *ch*

The Black K is in terrible straits. Black cannot fight
his assailants off, and therefore decides on a desperate
counter attack in order to draw the White forces
away from the pursuit of his K.

24 **Q x R**	**R–KKt1**
25 **P x P** *ch*	**K x P**
26 **B–Kt5**	Resigns

White threatens Q–Kt3. Black has no adequate defence against this, nor can he obtain sufficient counter-
attack.

KING'S GAMBIT DECLINED

WHITE: *Tschigorin* **BLACK:** *Marco*

1 **P–K4**	**P–K4**
2 **P–KB4**	**B–B4**

Black prefers development to the gain of the offered pawn.

3	Kt–KB3	P–Q3
4	B–B4	Kt–KB3
5	P–Q3	QKt–Q2

It is a peculiar manner of developing the QKt to place it in front of B and Q. The natural method is Kt–B3 or else B–K3, followed by QKt–Q2, or B3.

6	Kt–B3	P–B3
7	Q–K2	P–QKt4

Black, in playing on the wing, neglects the centre, but the centre is more important than either wing.

8	B–Kt3	P–QR4
9	P–QR4	P–Kt5
10	Kt–Q1	B–R3
11	P x P	. . . .

White opens lines in the centre by exchanging pawns which obstruct.

11	. . . .	P x P
12	Kt–K3	B x Kt
13	Q x B	. . . .

If 13 B x B ? Kt x P

13	. . . .	Kt–Kt5
14	Q–K2	O–O
15	B–Kt5	KKt–B3
16	O–O	P–R3
17	B–R4	Q–B2
18	Kt–Q2	Q–Q3
19	K–R1	. . . .

guarding against Q–Q5 ch, which would win the QKtP.

19	. . . .	P–Kt4

Black persistently manoeuvres on the wings. It was high time for him to strengthen his KBP by *19 . . .* R–R2, to follow this up by Kt–R2 and Kt–B4, so as to strengthen his weak points. The desultory attacks on temporary White weaknesses serve no purpose.

20	B–Kt3	K–Kt2
21	R–B5	Kt–KKt1
22	Kt–B1	QR–K1
23	Kt–K3	Q–Kt3
24	QR–KB1	P–B3

The White pieces have taken up positions firm and effectual at the same time.

25	P–R4	Kt–B4
26	P–R5	Q–R2
27	B–QB4	B–B1
28	Q–B2	Kt–K3

Black wants to place the Kt on the strongly fortified KB5, so as to block the White QB, but White, in now undertaking a violent onslaught, does not allow him the opportunity.

29	R x KP !	P x R
30	B x P *ch*	Kt–B3
31	Kt–Kt4	Kt–B5
32	Q–R7 *ch*	K–R1
33	B x Kt *ch*	Resigns

GIUOCO PIANO

WHITE: *Schiffers*	BLACK: *Harmonist*
1 P–K4	P–K4
2 Kt–KB3	Kt–QB3

3 B–B4	B–B4
4 P–B3	Kt–B3
5 P–Q4	P x P
6 P x P	B–Kt5 *ch*
7 B–Q2	B x B *ch*
8 QKt x B	P–Q4
9 P x P	KKt x P
10 Q–Kt3	QKt–K2

If *10* . . . , Kt–R4; *11* Q–R4 *ch*, P–B3; *12* B x Kt, Q x B; *13* O–O, O–O; *14* KR–K1 or QR–B1 and White has the advantage.

11 O–O	O–O
12 KR–K1	P–QB3
13 P–QR4	. . . .

This makes the position of the B secure.

13	Q–B2
14 QR–B1	. . . .

This threatens *15* B x Kt, Kt x B, *16* Q x Kt.

14	Kt–B5
15 Kt–Kt5	Kt(K2)–Kt3
16 R–K8	. . . .

This move pins the Rook which guards the KBP, the sole defence of the King.

16	R x R

Black must run this risk. Anything else would lose an important pawn.

17 B x P *ch*	K–R1

Not K–B1; *18* Kt x P *ch*, K–K2; *19* R–K1 *ch*

18 B x R	Kt–K7 *ch*
19 K–R1	Kt x R
20 Kt–B7 *ch*	K–Kt1

21	**Kt–R6** *dbl ch*	**K–B1**
22	**Q–Kt8** *ch*	**K–K2**
23	**B x Kt**	**P x B**
24	**Q x P** *ch*	**K–Q1**
25	**Q–B8** *ch*	**K–Q2**

The Black K now obstructs his B, and therefore also blocks the R. This is the right moment for developing inactive force, because Black now cannot do so.

26	**Kt–K4**	**Q–Q1**
27	**Q–Q6** *ch*	**K–K1**
28	**Kt–B6** *ch*	Resigns

These games, with their notes, indicate to the reader the manner in which he has to play over and to criticise the games of masters or of his friends. His criticism naturally has to be objective, both in praise and in dissent. The main task of criticism is to discover mistakes committed, in particular the mistake responsible for the result of the game. Notes to games should never be taken for granted, because the function of notes is to elucidate disputed points, and they must therefore appeal to the understanding. The habit of trying to comprehend notes makes a self-reliant chess player, and contributes to the development of judicious self-reliance, a valuable asset in life.

TASKS FOR THE STUDENT

TASK ONE:

White to move and win

TASK TWO:

White to win

TASK THREE:

Black to move and draw

TASK FOUR:

White to move and win

TASK FIVE:

White, with or without the move, draws

TASK SIX:

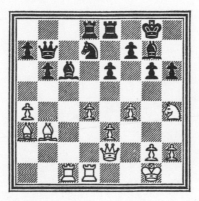

White smashes the K side by P–B5
Show this to be so

TASK SEVEN:

How would you win as White

TASK EIGHT:

How would you win as White

TASK NINE

How would you win as White

FINAL POSITIONS

Each of the following positions offers the opportunity of concluding the game by a series of forcing moves (a "combination"). Attempt to discover the right line of play. Analyse the moves of strong effect directed against vital weaknesses, because that analysis suggests the correct move.

Black: Janowski

White: Mason, to play

1 Q–R8 *ch*	K–Q2
2 Kt–Q4 !	R x R
3 Q x R	R x Q
4 R x R	K–B2 !
5 Kt x Q *ch*	K x R
6 Kt–Q4	K–B2
7 P–Kt4	

White has sufficient advantage in the end game to force the win by methodical advance by his King.

Black: Janowski

White: Dr. Tarrasch, to play

1 K–Q4	K–Kt6

If *1* . . . , R–B4; *2* K–K4, R x KtP; *3* P–B7, R–Kt5 *ch*; *4* K–K3, R–Kt6 *ch*; *5* K–B2 wins. Also *4* K–B3, R–Kt8; *5* K–B2 wins.

2 K–K5	K–B5
3 P–Kt6	R–K8 *ch*
4 K–Q6	R–KKt8
5 P–Kt7	K–Q5

If now 6 P–B7?, **R–Kt3** *ch*; 7 K moves, R x P draws.

6	**K–B6**	**K–B5**
7	**K–Q7**	**K–Q4**
8	**K–K8**	**K–K3**
9	**P–B7**	**R–QR8**
10	**P–B8(Kt)** *ch*	**K moves**
11	**P–Kt8** queens and wins.	

Put up positions of strong effect and large mobility and experiment with them; you will then be able to discover surprising combinations and train your judgment in respect of them.

Black: Bogoljubow

White: Reti, to play and win

Write out some of the scores of some of your games and comment upon them. Attempt before all to discover the last mistake committed, because that one is directly responsible for the result. Let your method be that of trying, judicious trying, often repeated.

White to play and win

The writing of notes is an art of which the notes in this book convey no clear conception: they have been written for the purpose of methodical teaching. Notes to masterly games addressed to a public of connoisseurs are subject to a different standard. Your effort in commenting upon games cannot attain to excellence except after many trials, but it conduces to the forming of your judgment and your taste. Before all, learn to be critical. Many notes published in books, chess columns and chess magazines are misleading. I cannot go into this question fully here, but let us take as a specimen a game from one of the most celebrated matches, that between McDonnell and Labourdonnais, annotated by Paul Morphy, who beat all the masters of his time brilliantly.

The following diagram and notes are quoted from "Morphy Gleanings," recently published by Mr. Philip W. Sergeant. The whole of the note following Black's 37th move is by Paul Morphy:

Position after Black's 36th move

Black: Labourdonnais

White: McDonnell

37 **P–R5**

Very well played.

37 . . . . **Q–R3**

R x Q would have won a piece, but could not have
saved the game. Suppose *37* . . . , R x Q; *38* P x Q,
Kt x B (or *a*); *39* R x Kt, R x R; *40* P–B6, and will
easily queen one of his Ps. (*a*) *38* . . . , R x B; *39*
R x R, Kt x R; *40* P–K6 (best), Kt–K5 (best); *41*
P–K7, Kt–B3 (best); *42* P–Kt4, K–B1 (best); *43*
P x RP (best), P x RP (best). (The line of play beginning with White's 43rd move is the only road to
victory. Should he move *43* P–Kt5, Black would draw
by BP x P, and, on White's capturing the Kt, moving
K–Q2. We recommend this study to the student's attention; it will amply repay perusal); *44* P–Kt7 *ch*
(best), K x P. (Here again, should White incautiously
advance P–Kt5, Black would secure a drawn battle

by P x P, and moving K–Q2 on P x Kt); *45* P–Kt5, Kt–K1. (The advance of the KtP now forces the game, the Black K having been removed one square by the sacrifice of the QKtP); *46* P–B6, winning.

White might also have won by *40* P–B6, but not so prettily. These variations contain a number of others which we must omit, after commending them to the patient study of amateurs.

38	B–Q2	Q–R6
39	Q–B1	R–Kt1
40	P–B6	Q–R4
41	P–B7	R–KB1
42	P–K6	Kt–Kt6
43	Q–B3	Q–R8 *ch*
44	K–B2	Kt–K5 *ch*
45	K–K2	Q–QKt8
46	P–K7	Q x P *ch*
47	Q–Q3	Kt–Kt6 *ch*
48	K–Q1	Resigns.

30th game of the match series.

This analysis, so beautiful and convincing at White's 37th move, fails to notice the exceeding importance of Black's 38th move. Black certainly committed a very grave error there. Labourdonnais, fatigued by Mc-Donnell's stout resistance, which in those days no other master would have been capable of rendering, chose a line of attack that hampered the mobility of his Rook and so lost an all-important move. He should have placed his Q either on KR2, where it stood firm and menacing because its range threatened directly and indirectly the K, the KBP, the Q and the R, or on KR4, a position sufficiently strong and fine to recommend that move although not so strong as the former. In reply to *38* . . . Q–R4, White has to reply *39* B–K3, with the possible continuation *39* P x P; *40* R–B2; or *40* P–B6, R–Kt1; *41* K–B1. Against *38* . . . Q–R2, White has the choice between *39* B–K3, P x P; *40* R–B2, Kt x R; *41* K x Kt, R–Kt5, which leaves the KBP pinned and the K exposed; or *39* Q–B1, R–Kt1; *40* Q–B3, Kt–Kt6, when White probably would try the desperate course *41* P–B6.

The position is interesting and instructive. Let my pupil take board and men and try its varied possibilities. After a little while he will himself perceive the moves, strong and weak, alluring but faulty, simple or profound, which in this position present themselves. By making the analysis myself and informing him of its definite results I should deprive him of a splendid opportunity. Results are of less account than Methods. Let him acquire the method of judicious trials which will stand him in good stead in many ways. Even the little that has been said demonstrates the error committed by Labourdonnais and the grievous omission of the annotator.

In the literature accessible to me, some of which is quite modern, I have not detected criticism on Black's 38th move, although it appears to be the decisive mistake. This deficiency is so much more deplorable as the games between McDonnell and Labourdonnais, played a century ago, have attracted world-wide attention. We have now a hundred players who would

prefer *38* . . . Q–R2 or Q–R4 to Q–R6 unhesitatingly.
In the belief in authority there is a drug that causes
those who have partaken of it to renounce their judgment.

For education in self-reliance, facts of the above
type, if properly attended to, are of value. You have
to gain experience of this kind to enable you to find a
suitable mean between humble acceptance of the dicta
of authority and overbearing self-assertion. Chess provides you with such opportunities, because you can
prove propositions in chess, if need be by checkmating
your opponent, whereas in other fields of endeavour
it is difficult for you to obtain a hearing or to prove
your case, even though you may be the champion of
Truth. This analysis is not aimed against Paul Morphy. His was a creative mind but too far ahead of his
period to give of his best. That period blindly believed
in authority; it was eager to pay genius by uncritical
praise, but slow to pay its debt in other ways. By your
effort to acquire critical judgment you help to make
your period cognisant of the rightful claims of genius.

THE CHESS WORLD

Any chess player who ceases to play the game merely for his private amusement, but desires to probe the mysteries of chess as it progresses and to enjoy the art of the great masters, thereby *ipso facto* becomes a denizen of the chess world.

That institution is alive as long as the game of chess is pregnant with unsolved problems. Its task is to lift little by little the veil from the unknown and to spread an understanding of and a sound taste for chess. This task has its reward. The good things somehow resemble each other, and the bad things likewise. Emerson said that a drop of water mirrors the whole universe. He who does one worthy thing with the ambition of an artist is incapable of lack of respect for any other worthy cause.

The task has also its responsibilities. He who undertakes it must be alive to its opportunities, and to its dangers. If not he will fail, and history will ask him why he undertook a task for which he was not fitted, and one which others would have striven to do for Art's sake.

The mainspring of progress is the creative master,

it is his genius which produces what is new in the sense that it was never comprehended before. It is his art which inspires and by uniting the many diverse units of the chess world, makes a body with but one will. His name is remembered throughout the centuries, and his masterpieces acquire depth and brilliance. His mind needs the spur of competition. No great work can be done without passion and necessity. True genius is quite unconscious of the fact. He has to encounter infinite resistance, to be capable of infinite power. Unless he meets an opponent of his own rank his style deteriorates just as a cultivated plant which is not tended reverts to its wild state. A great task set him by an enthusiastic multitude overcomes this natural tendency and lifts him beyond himself.

If, like Philidor, a master is in a class by himself, he never attains to his maturity, but such a condition does not prevail for any length of time. A new generation will arise inspired with a new fervour. Generally, therefore, each epoch produces a multitude of creative masters. Each of them has a style which bears the impress of his individuality, and their styles differ in essentials. Non-creative masters are all alike because they are mere copyists. Creative masters differ greatly because that is the hall-mark of individuality and enterprise. The road that leads through known regions is clearly delineated, but in unknown territories the road has yet to be mapped out and paved, and the pioneers penetrating there try different directions.

It is this tension between the creative masters that lends colour and interest to their struggle. Each of them has his adherents. Opinions clash, discussions arise, a curiosity to know which of them is the strongest excites the multitude. That is the time and condition for a match or a tournament. The organiser has to recognise that condition and to profit by it. He himself should not take sides. Impartiality and justice must be his law. In that spirit of fairness he has to prepare the contest. If the tension between the styles of the great masters, instead of being fructified, is allowed to run to waste, if mediocrity is favoured, if the inarticulate yearning of the multitude is left unsatisfied, the organisers are at fault. In such a period many mediocre games are produced, but their large number does not compensate the chess world for its loss of artistic games. Such a period confers no glory, nor does it last long. A new generation resolutely sweeps aside the period of mediocrity, to make room for something worth while.

In what period do we live? There are creative masters but the organisation of the chess world does not produce competition between them. The master is discouraged by the prevailing system. "There is something rotten in the state of Denmark."

It is the task of the future historian to speak the final word on this issue. At any rate sound feeling will prevail *in the end*, because mediocre works cannot arouse enthusiasm and are doomed to be forgotten. They produce by contrast an appetite for what is good and wholesome. The future therefore belongs to the creative master and to an organisation which works in unison with him.